# YOUR KNOWLEDGE HAS VALUE

- We will publish your bachelor's and
  master's thesis, essays and papers

- Your own eBook and book -
  sold worldwide in all relevant shops

- Earn money with each sale

Upload your text at www.GRIN.com
and publish for free

# How does AI impact the organizational identity in client-focused investment advisory?

Moritz Merklinger

**Bibliographic information published by the German National Library:**

The German National Library lists this publication in the National Bibliography; detailed bibliographic data are available on the Internet at http://dnb.dnb.de.

ISBN: 9783346720566
This book is also available as an ebook.

© GRIN Publishing GmbH
Nymphenburger Straße 86
80636 München

Print and binding: Books on Demand GmbH, Norderstedt, Germany
Printed on acid-free paper from responsible sources.

The present work has been carefully prepared. Nevertheless, authors and publishers do not incur liability for the correctness of information, notes, links and advice as well as any printing errors.

GRIN web shop: https://www.grin.com/document/1274271

1

**Abstract**

It is evident that an employee's fundamental work may shift when working with a decision-making, self-learning and intelligent AI. It is also conceivable that the employee's own values or work identity may adjust to the AI in some way. But what about when you do not just analyze the individual consultant? If you look at the broader context and analyze the change in values and identity of the organization as a whole. To understand how the values and identity of the individual, but more importantly the identity of an organization, are affected by the introduction of AI, we interviewed, coded and analyzed 5 asset managers from one of Germany's leading cooperative banks. Based on our research, we show that while the introduction of AI has a major impact on the way advisors work, it has little to almost no impact on the identity of the organization.That this may have something to do with the scope of application of AI in the institution and the value stability of the bank will be discussed in more detail later in the paper. With our study, we join the existing research on the topic of AI changing organizational identity.

# 1 Introduction

Technological progress is driving us forward and constantly and continuously changing our working world, our leisure time and our entire everyday life. If you look back to earlier times when people did not have their own telephone, let alone internet access, our working world now looks very different. The majority of professionals work and communicate digitally. (Faraj et al., 2018) from home. This proportion has increased massively, especially in the era of Corona. (Beineke, 2020). Software solutions such as Teams or Zoom have already changed the way we communicate. But learning algorithms are changing our working world even more intensively than some other simpler software programmes. This is also supported by Lee et al., 2015), who emphasize that algorithms optimize or take over the work of various professions. We can see that this is already in full swing in our own research topic. But does the AI we are discussing have as strong an impact as the following postulates? "Futurists predict that a third of jobs that exist today could be taken by Smart Technology, Artificial Intelligence, Robotics, and Algorithms (STARA) by 2025" (Brougham & Haar, 2018, S. 1) This statement will be especially true in industries that produce an enormous amount of information, but on which their core business also depends. This is because machine self-learning algorithms are able to better and more efficiently evaluate much larger amounts of data more quickly, while also educating themselves.(Brynjolfsson & Mitchell, 2017) Among the reasons why this type of information system is used are, for example, the reduction of costs as well as the increase in economic profits and thus increased productivity(Harvard Business Review Press, 2019) (Brynjolfsson & McAfee, 2014).

However, while there are many positives to be gained, it is important to note that organizations and professions are currently challenged by AI (Barley et al., 2017) (Faraj et al 2018). Specifically, the focus on organizational identity may be worthwhile, as AI has become a central theme in theorizing about myriad dimensions of work and organizational life (Bailey et al. 2012; Orlikowski 2010; Zammuto et al. 2007). But besides influencing organizational identity, there is also the difficulty and challenge of figuring out what tasks the learning algorithms can take on, how this affects the work environment, and most importantly, how the organization and workers deal with the tension regarding the interconnectedness between humans and machines (Faraj et al., 2018).

The question emerges to what extent an introduced AI influences its environment. This can be various fields. In our specific case, we focus on the organizational identity of a bank. Since there is not yet much research on this, we will pursue the following research question: how the implementation of an AI influences the organizational identity in customer-focused financial advisory services. But what exactly is understood by the term organizational identity. In short, organizational identity provides information about what differentiates the organization from others, what is considered central to the organization, and what enduring characteristics an organization has (Whetten, 2006).

Our research builds on Ashfort and Whetten's definition of organizational identity and relates to identity change. In order to identify a possible shift in this organizational identity, we include 5 interviews from the banking industry that could have perceived a possible shift due to the introduction of AI.

First, we will define the term organizational identity and artificial intelligence. Then we will go into our case description as well as the data collection and data analysis. Finally, we will present our collected data and interpret it in the last step.
Through our research, we were able to determine that the implementation of AI has triggered a change in the way of working in asset management, but that it is too insignificant to influence the organizational identity of the bank.

## 2 Theory

### 2.1 Artificial Intelligence

In the following section, Artificial Intelligence, abbreviated to AI, is discussed in more detail.

AI technology has a long history that is actively and constantly changing and growing. Scientists have been working on artificial intelligence since the middle of the last century. Their goal: to engineer machines that learn and think like humans. ((Shrestha et al., 2019)) Hereinafter, a brief historical synopsis of milestones in the technology and research.

The birth of the term Artificial Intelligence can be traced back to 1956. At that time, a conference on artificial intelligence was held at Dartmouth College, this conference has since been considered the kick-off of research. For a long time, however, there was no groundbreaking innovation or research on Artificial Intelligence. But AI saw its big boom in 1997 when, for the first time, a computer outperformed the then world chess champion. From that point on, further development proceeded rapidly.(von Krogh, 2018, S. 404)

Nowadays, it is difficult to imagine life without AI, whether in legal proceedings or in the automotive industry (Ramsey, 2015) or, as in our example, in the banking industry, AI is used in incredibly many ways.

AIs perform highly complex searches, analyses and processes that involve logical reasoning (von Krogh, 2018, S. 1) including in open-source frameworks, application programming interfaces (APIs), drag and drop tools to create custom KIM models, and also in governance activities. (Constantinides , 2019). Basically, entire tasks previously performed by humans are now perfectly emulated and taken over by AI (Faraj et al., 2018)(Davenport and Kirby 2016). AIs need a feed of error-free data to draw error-free predictions, to evolve and thus to undergo an independent and continuous learning process(von Krogh, 2018) (Krogh) (Davenport & Kirby, 2016;) In this context, artificial intelligence is defined as algorithms and computer-based systems that recognise patterns of behaviour from past data sets and incorporate these patterns in the future. (Lebovitz after Krogh) (von Krogh, 2018)

In conclusion, despite many years of meticulous research, the development of Artificial Intelligence is still very much in its infancy and human thinking is still elusive (Barley et al., 2017)

**2.2 Organizational Identity**

In order to be amenable to examine the extent to which the implementation of artificial intelligence influences organizational identity, this identity must be defined and declared. According to Ashfort (2020), OI is defined by differentiating the parameters "who" and "what" on the basis of the unitary entity, conjoint entity and aggregation of members. Another attempt to define OI is to distinguished between ideational, definitional and phenomenological dimensions, which will be examined and differentiated in more detail (Tyworth, 2014). These two examples are representative for a lot of other ways of description possibilities. A unified definition does not exist but in the following we will go back to the origin. The starting point of the research on organizational identity was a previously paper by Albert and Whetten in 1985. From that time on, research on this topic gained more and more popularity and majority of the subsequent papers refer to the basic concept of the previously mentioned authors. (Tripsas, 2009)

Albert und Whetten describe organizational identity as the following.

"(a) what is taken by organization members to be central to the organization; (b) what makes the organization distinctive from other organizations (…); and (c) what is perceived by members to be an enduring or continuing feature linking the present organization with the past ( and presumably the future)"( Albert& Whetten, 1985,p.264)

Organizational identity consists of those elements that are perceived by employees as central and enduring in an organization and that enable it to be distinguished from other organizations. In this respect, they base their conceptualizations of organizational identity predominantly on psychological theories of identity. (Whetten 2007; Whetten & Mackey, 2002). This presupposes that organizations are seen as social actors with almost the same rights and duties as individuals. (Scott 2001). In this regard, organizations are not seen as a sum of individuals, rather they are conceived as an autonomous organism and as a distinct unit. The treatment of the organization as if it constituted a distinct individual can be traced back to the concept of anthropomorphism "an attribution of human qualities or behavior to nonhuman entities, objects, and events (Ashforth et al., 2020, S. p.?). The intention is to allow a social rational and particularly emotional identification of the workers with the organization as well as a "psychological contract" between the two parties. Ashfort and Shinoff assert that anthropomorphism enables organizational members to conceive of their organization in terms of "who it is / who we are as an organization" (e.g., personality, attitudes, affects) rather than in terms of "what it is / what we are e.g., industry, structure, age)

## 3 Research Method

### 3.1 Case Description

The results in this paper were obtained in cooperation with one specific Branch of a German cooperative bank. The entire banking community comprises approximately 800 branches, 138,000 employees, 18.4 million members and achieved a balance sheet total of 1,029 billion euros (2020).

The algorithm discussed in this academic paper is provided by one of the partner banks. Briefly described, this data-based algorithm is used in the stock advisory service for private clients and works as outlined below. This advisory tool is nourished by various data sources, which are both digital and human. The digital data source is provided by the in-house AI called Malina (Machine Learning for Investment Applications) and concentrates on the performance of markets, asset classes or company sectors. The AI is fuelled with data that, in the opinion of investment managers, are pertinent to stock market movements. In addition to exchange rate movements and the development of commodity prices, this also includes the shape of the yield curve. Based on these data, the AI creates a forest of decision trees and can furthermore match these data to historical events and incorporate them into the underlying calculations. In this manner, the AI can not only forecast the probability of which assets will change and how but is also simultaneously trained for future occasions. The human data source, in this case the client and advisor, does not focus particularly on the performance of the mutual funds, but on how well which fund fits the client's intended strategy best. In a client meeting, the client is guided by the advisor through a click path that asks for all relevant data for the AI analysis. In addition to risk tolerance, this data also includes environmental awareness, savings rate, investment duration and other customer-related information. Based on this information, the AI then assigns the customer to one of 6 different risk classes. These are as follows:

- Low risk
- Moderate risk
- Increased risk
- High risk
- Very high risk

Based on this, the advisor is provided with very promising funds that are compatible with the client's strategy and risk class.

The programme, which was introduced in late 2020, has so far only been available to advisors, but also enables deals to be closed via online meetings. By simplifying the consultation and visualization options, the consultants can not only advise clients faster and more efficiently, but also address new clients who are still inexperienced in the area of value investments. The AI thus allows for more cost-efficient work as well as the exploration of new target groups.

**3.2 Data Collection**

In order to ensure the most accurate data possible, the data collection was conducted using semi-structured interviews. This not only provides in-depth insights into complex human behaviors, but also allows leeway for both open and spontaneous questions as well as answers from the interviewers and interviewees. Through set questions about position and duration in the organization as well as own personal values, a fixed framework is given in which the moderators but also the interviewee could spontaneously disclose his or her independent experience and opinion. The interviewees all come from the field of private asset management for high-net-worth private clients and had already worked with this AI. In order to gather diverse opinions, the interview participants differentiated themselves by age, position and work experience (Appendix 1). All of the interviews took place in early June 2021, lasted between 25 minutes and 40 minutes and were conducted almost exclusively by both interview partners. In total, we were able to survey 5 interview partners and record a rough duration of 2 hours 30 minutes of audio material.

### 3.3 Data analysis

In attempting to systematically analyze and structure our interview data, we decided to apply the technique of Gioia. Particularly in a qualitative study, organizing the data by 1st and 2nd order concepts delivers valuable glimpses into the theory of the data. The objective of coding is to find concepts and phenomena that explain and underpin the findings of the research.

In order to identify the 1st order concepts, we initially coded the interviews. In doing so, we reached a total of 204 original statements. From these original statements we compiled 50 1st Order Concepts and consolidated them in the next step into 9 2nd Order Concepts. In the last step, we assigned 3 supergroups to each of the 2nd Order Concepts, which finally formed the Aggregated Dimensions. To assure the quality of our coding, both seminar participants coded independently of each other and fused the results into a document at the end. The result and our model can be found in Appendix II.

### 4. Results
### 4.1 Organizational Identity

In accordance with the approach of Ashfort (2020), we have attempted to find out how the organizational identity of a bank can be defined by asking questions relating to the three dimensions. To achieve this, we have broken down 64 original statements into 24 1st order concepts and grouped them into 3 2nd order concepts. The 2nd order concepts are equal to the three dimensions, are as follows and are explained and put into relation on the following pages.

- Anthropomorphism
- Organisational values
- Individual Values

### 4.1.1 Anthropomorphism

Starting with anthropomorphism, this is an attribution of human qualities or behavior to non-human entities, objects, and events (Ashforth et al., 2020, p.? as cited in Epley, Waytz, Cacioppo, 2007; Guthrie,1993).

Here, the consultants were asked to assign human attributes to their company. We were able to identify a total of 15 original statements and define 6 1st Order Concepts. For example, the bank was described as an older but experienced person. In addition, the person strives to keep up with the times so as not to get stale. ("A more mature age with experience and still trying to implement new things, not to get rusty". IP5)

In line with the bank's advanced age and experience, the humane characteristics of the bank are also characterized by their independence ("And yet every single bank wants to remain independent." IP3). But in addition to the self-referential characteristics, the bank is also characterized by its community spirit ("And I would say that the biggest thing is the strong community, [...]." IP3) and the "[family] appearance" (IP2, IP3).

### 4.1.2 Organizational Values

Now that we have the bank with the anthropomorphic characteristics of being elderly, experienced but also family-oriented, we have to attribute values to this person, this bank, this organization, for which it wants to embody. It is conspicuous that we have almost twice as many original statements for the organizational values, a total of 30 original statements, than for the anthropomorphic ones. These were combined into a total of 12 1st order concepts. It may also be observed that each of the interviewees could state at least 4 or more values that refer to the organization. But most noteworthy is that the bank has firmly anchored 10 values, which it also communicates officially. These are as follows:

> [...] regionally rooted, objective, trustworthy, competent, independent, at eye level, crisis-proof, resilient, fair, partnership-based. These are the 10 values we have given ourselves. (IP2)

This in itself not only constitutes a framework of values to which staff, members and clients can orient themselves, rather it also shows how value-based this bank is. However, in addition to the official values, every advisor has been able to ascribe further values to the bank, which go over and above what has already been outlined.

Although it was not included in the official values, the cooperative (IP1, IP2) was mentioned in 5 original statements and it was even mentioned that the founders of the bank had written the cooperative on their banner ("The [Bank] come from the cooperative sector, of course. And the cooperative sector, well, I say, that's how the founders are, have written it on their banner." IP1) and it thus also becomes a "unique selling point compared to the competition" (IP2).

In conjunction with this legal form, there was also an explicit focus on customer and member prioritization. In 14 statements, it was emphasized that the well-being of members and customers "in all states of life" (IP4) comes first. ("Because our main focus is of course with our members, always [...] committed." IP4). Members are thus treated "fairly" (IP2), "in partnership" (IP1) and at "eye level" (IP4). Therefore, these attributes are also to be seen as a value and part of the identity of the bank we are examining.

> But that you also want to deal with our customers and members as partners and at eye level, and that you also want to advise them in this way, so I'll just say as partners at eye level. [...] That is actually the approach of [the bank]. (IP1)

But the bank's local solidarity is not just hollow words either. This is not only evidenced by 4 original statements, but also by the way in which these regional ties are practiced. When repair work or members' meetings are due, for example, orders are placed with the craftsman or butcher around the corner. Local associations are supported, and the bank is also present at schools.

> Yes. I think you may have experienced it yourself when you were at school or clubs. It's just always the case that the local [banks] made gifts of money, gifts in kind, donations. [...] That means we work together with our customers, with companies and craftsmen, and a part of it goes back to the members through dividends. Or, of course, we now also support a lot of craftsmen by saying that if we have orders for bank buildings or other things, then we get local craftsmen involved in the classic way, of course, or we buy butchers from the local baker, if we have any members' meetings, we support associations (IP4).

After consistently positive characteristics, however, one characteristic stands out negatively through 2 statements. Ironically, this is the innovative capacity of this bank. It is said that it is not "ahead of the rest" (IP5) and that it is "one of the least innovative banking groups" (IP3). The introduction of AI has nothing to do with innovation but is rather "the last possible step in order to still come close to reaching those customers who are exactly into such things. [...] The only protection not to lose more [customers]." (IP3).

### 4.1.3 Individual Values

To wrap up the three levels of organizational identity, we take a closer look at the last level, individual values of the respective consultants. By clustering 19 original statements into 6 1st order concepts, we have the opportunity to find individual characteristics as well as overlaps with the organizational values.

To begin with, we can confirm that the advisors, with reference to themselves, can absolutely identify with the values of the bank (IP1, IP2, IP3, IP5). These include "Cooperative, family and member oriented." (IP2). IP1 also emphasizes the cooperative structure in particular. ("I wouldn't be in this [...] structure for so long now if I didn't stand behind it. I like this cooperative idea." IP1). In addition, the regional factor is also lived individually. ("I live [...] 100m away from the bank, so you can always find me" IP5).

But the counsellors do not only see this support for the values in themselves, they also see the identification with the values in their colleagues. IP3 was able to assure us that there are colleagues who not only personify the organizational values, but also practice them. ("There are certainly quite, quite a lot of people who embody them and also live them out." IP3).

With a focus on the individual values, however, a broader portfolio of values emerges. For example, IP3, in contrast to the bank, describes itself as "innovative" and IP4, "not averse to technical progress". This is therefore the first, but also the only absolutely contradictory value that occurs between the individual and organizational levels.

However, the range of values is enlarged in detail by the points "reliability" (IP4) and profit orientation, which is aimed at the customer, the bank and IP5 itself. ("I then always try [...] to create a winning model. That is, the bank should benefit, the client, but also me." IP5)

But one can also attribute conscientiousness and a sense of duty to them. ("I try [...], when I meet these people on the street, to be able to look them in the eye" IP5).

To put it in a nutshell, it can be said that the composition of the three dimensions, anthropomorphism, organizational values and individual values, results in an identity of the company that is characterized by cooperativeness, regionality and customer focus. These values are embodied and acted upon both internally, in this case the identification of the advisors with the bank, and externally, in the customer advisory services themselves.

### 4.2 Identity Changes

Having shown what, the bank as an organization and the advisors as individuals stand for, we can now analyze how the values of the bank have changed through the use of AI in client-focused wealth banking. For a more reliable analysis, we have identified a total of

24 original statements, grouped them into 11 1st order concepts and, in the next step, grouped them into 3 2nd order concepts. The 2nd order concepts are

- positive alternations
- negative alternations
- no alternations

They depict the possible shifts in organizational identity that have been triggered by AI.

### 4.2.1 Positive alternations

Positive alternations are defined as whether the introduction of AI has resulted in new positive values or enhanced existing values. Eventually, whether the organizational identity of the bank has been positively influenced.

With a total of only 4 original statements and a 1st order concept,

- strengthening customer benefits

it is clear that the AI has only a minor to non-existent positive effect on the bank's organizational identity. The only point that is positively emphasized is that one has "another possibility to do something good for the customer" (IP5). According to IP5, this also results in improved customer loyalty. ("If it works, he will come back" IP5). Admittedly, at first glance this almost seems as if it were not worth mentioning. But if you take a further look at the individual and organizational values, you realise the importance of the focus on the customer. Thus, the AI does not hit the broad mass of values, but it matches exactly the value that is considered extremely important by the organization as well as by the individual consultant.

What needs to be mentioned at this point is that in the later part of the paper, further positive changes through AI will be discussed. There, however, the focus is on the type of counselling and not on the organizational identity.

### 4.2.2 Negative alternations

Negative alternations are defined as whether the introduction of AI has created new negative values or worsened existing values. Finally, whether the organizational identity of the bank has been negatively affected.

With a total of 7 original statements and 2 1st order concepts, it can be seen that the AI has a weak negative effect on the bank's organizational identity. Since one can assume that the officially communicated values (see 4.1.2 organizational values) but also the individually lived values (see 4.1.3 individual values) apply not only to customers and members but also to employees, one can interpret a negative shift in the values of partnership and fairness.

> The company does not develop further and does not manage to create new opportunities through free time but saves money without end. [...] It's always about the saving factor [...] making people redundant. [...] I also notice that the burden on each individual, especially in my area or in our bank, is getting bigger and bigger, because more and more is expected. And there is no time left to take a breath for half a day in order to deal with the innovations. Instead, here is the information, it has to work from tomorrow, and you have to use it. (IP3)

Although this is the opinion of a single consultant, it clearly shows that the ongoing implementation of AIs negatively affects the values already mentioned above. For it is neither partnership-based nor fair to let loyal employees ("[...] in September then 16 years" IP3) work in this negative working climate.

Even if the highly praised value of cooperativism is taken up again, the motive reflected here is saving, always "focusing more on efficiency" (IP3) and never-ending demands on employees, a clear loss of internal interaction with employees and a certain greed for profit, which no longer has much to do with corporativism.

However, it must also be put into perspective that this feedback came from IP3, who described himself as "innovative" and would like to see more consistent use of AI. Since this feedback did not come from anyone else, one can speculate that he misjudges his colleagues ("[...] especially in my area or at our bank [...]" (IP3)" or that only he himself has problems with it. Even if only weakly and with possibly only one person, the AI has caused a negative alternation.

### 4.2.3 No alternations

No alternations are defined as the bank's identity or values not having been negatively or positively alternated by the introduction of AI. Finally, the bank's organizational identity has not been affected.

Looking at the structure according to Gioia, a clear picture can already be seen. With 13 original statements and 9 1st order concepts, there is a significant preponderance compared to positive or negative alternations. This is also confirmed by the fact that each interview partner answered the question "whether the values have changed due to the introduction of AI [...]" (IPM) as follows.

- IP1: "Exactly, that is unchanged. The values remain the same."
- IP2: "I was just trying to think, this [AI] is after all a total product. And the other thing is a [...] corporate philosophy. In this respect [...] nothing can clash. But I haven't found anything that clashes now."
- IP3: "Therefore, I wouldn't say that it has changed."
- IP4: "No, [IPM], I don't see it that way now."
- IP5: "No, I wouldn't say that now."

As far as the future development of values is concerned, these are also so firmly anchored in the company that there is "rather [no] danger of them being endangered by this artificial intelligence" (IP2).

Thus, although there are mild alternations in the positive but also negative direction, the core values, regional rooting, communication at eye level and objectivity (see 4.1.2), to name just a few of the values, remain unaffected.

## 4.3 Consulting Changes

Through the semi-structured interviews, we not only had the chance to ask the consultants about their perception of a possible identity alteration, but through the open nature of the interview, we were able to obtain information that triggered an enormous change not in the identity, but in the basic work of consulting. Thus, consulting in this case is defined as describing the way of working with clients and AI. Consulting changes hence summarizes a change in the work.

With a total of 67 statements and 15 1st order concepts, we have developed the following 3 2nd order concepts

- Advantages
- Disadvantages
- Future Improvements

Which will allow us to discover further implications of AI not on the organizational value level but on the individual work level.

### 4.3.1 Advantages

With 45 statements out of a total of 66 statements in the aggregated dimension "Consulting Changes", it cannot be denied that this AI has a strong positive influence on wealth management advice for private clients. This starts with supposedly banal topics such as the visualization of shares.

> Because, of course, you can also show or represent something to the customer in a plastic way or on the screen. You can look at values in retrospect. You can look at developments together. How has the fund [developed] in the last 5 years, 6 years? (IP1)

In a positive sense, this entails a rat's tail. Because it "takes away the customers' fear" (IP2) of the stocks and you can appeal to customers who are "not interested in stocks" (IP1). Particularly with customers who are new to the field of stocks, this AI makes it possible for the advisors to provide the customers with a pleasant introduction. ("For customers who have not yet had any contact with the topic, this is perfect. For me, [the AI] is a gain." IP1)

But the "investment assistant" (IP1) does not only shine when addressing new customers. For 4 of the 5 advisors states that the AI allows them to work faster. This is then reflected in the fact that the advisor "can quickly advise the customer on 5 different structures and used to need [...] one or two hours of conversation for 5 structures." (IP3). This not only benefits the advisor's and client's time management, but also the investment portfolio.

> [...] the client can also change his investment strategy much, much faster. So if he says, I want [instead of] 30% shares now 70% in the future, I would have had to start a whole, whole new counselling documentation in the old world and now I can just change the whole thing with one click if the client releases [it] for himself. (IP3)

With the term "counselling documentation" we also pick up on another important point right away. This is a "legal framework that has become stronger and stronger over time." (IP1). This is defined in more detail below by the information source IHK Lüneburg.

Since 2010, investment service providers, mostly banks and other financial service providers, have been subject to a documentation obligation for their employees who professionally recommend the purchase or sale of shares, certificates or other stocks. This must be documented in writing and contains the following points:

- Reason for the advice
- Duration of the advisory meeting
- The circumstances of the client on which the advice is based
- The client's concerns and the desired weighting of the investment

- All recommendations made in the course of the discussion as well as the main reasons.

Before the transaction is concluded, the client must receive the signed transcript from the advisor. (IHK Lüneburg-Wolfsburg)

The aim of this law is that advisors "speak to the client as transparently as possible so as not to get into [...] liability issues." (IP1)

So, if you have a counselling session nowadays, the counsellor has to document everything for his own protection. This costs time not only during but also after the discussion and is "empty business [...] and lost time for client and advisor" (IP3). The AI enters this interface in a labour-saving and liability-limiting way.

> I have no documentation obligation here, because the customer answers my every question with support, and I have the click track. [...] Application comes out. I go through the application with the client. I send it off if he wants to do it and he gets the application. (IP1)

However, in addition to the benefits just mentioned, the counsellors also mentioned additional positive change in terms of the accuracy of the counselling. For example, this offers a "more targeted implementation" (IP5), as one "rambles less left and right" (IP5) and is thus "faster and more effective on the way" (IP5)

### 4.3.2 Disadvantages

However, like every coin, this one also has its flip side. But a closer look reveals that these are by far not as significant as the advantages, with only 9 statements.

For example, IP1 and IP4 complain that this AI is a fixed construct without flexibility.

> Yes, of course it is always a rigid [...] procedure. This is how it works, from to. [...] With individual funds I can just say, [...] I can exclude this or include this and that. (IP4)

This means that the advisors cannot select an "individual solution, like now specifically an individual stock" (IP1). This AI can only offer funds from various investment areas and is thus "purely a mixed story." (IP1).

Furthermore, there is also a disadvantage in the relationship between the client and the advisor.

Through automation, the client actually only has to contact the advisor once during the advisory meeting. Once the investment is finalized, nothing else is required.

For those who have something like this in place today, the frequency of contact is basically reduced. This means that the clients have no other wishes for the bank or the advisor. There will be silence for a while. (IP2)

This is also accompanied by the fact that "you lose the customer as far as the personal aspect is concerned". (IP3) According to IP3, this is because "many different processes [...] are no longer regulated internally by the [advisor], but by the AI [...]". As a result, the customer thinks he is interacting with the advisor, whereas it is only the AI and "then it takes the human element out of it" (IP3).

Another relevant point, which was only mentioned by one advisor, is the notion of technology-averse colleagues. IP3 sees a challenge because "the employees [...] are not capable of working [if you] can't deal with [the AI]". This creates the danger that "the [tech-averse] will be left behind." This problem not only can affect the morale and motivation of the consultant, but in the long run it also affects the quality delivered to the clients. However, as IP3 describes himself as innovative and relates this problem more to his colleagues, this point can be expected to have little to no effect on identity.

### 4.3.3 Future Improvements for Consulting

Despite the consultants' high level of satisfaction with the AI, in their opinion the tool has not yet reached full maturity and still offers room for improvement. This is also evidenced by our coding of the interviews. We identified a total of 13 statements from all 5 consultants and combined them into 6 1st order concepts.

A fundamental demand, which coincides with the high level of approval for AI, is that the topic of AI and automation should be pushed further.

The bank or the company always has to make sure that it stays on the ball. They have to have the latest products or artificial intelligence support tools at hand and not stand still, i.e. keep up with the technology. (IP1)

The specific wish is that it should be "brought very strongly to the masses" (IP2) and that it should be "used much more [...] and more consistently everywhere where it is possible." (IP3).

Another point, which was already described in 4.3.2, is that the system is a fixed construct without flexibility.

> The desired state, as already mentioned, would be to have even more flexibility. To offer shares, savings plans, ETFs, in other words really everything that is on the free market, in the sense of the customer. We are not yet able to offer that on a broad scale. (IP5)

However, this does not only apply to the broad range of products on the free market, but also to processes that the AI is not yet capable of. For example, it is criticised that when the customer decides on a product and "wants to move on to the next strategy in the next step" (IP1), this cannot happen immediately afterwards. The advisor "has to wait [...] at least half an hour [...]" (IP1). Thus, there is also the legitimate criticism from IP3 that he has to become even faster. This can also go hand in hand with the desire for a "leaner process" (IP4).

Finally, there was isolated criticism from the counsellors that it needs to become more pragmatic (IP2) and that one should "get rid of forms [...] altogether" (IP2). There is also a desire for there to be "no more technical problems" (IP1). In addition, the process is also inflated by the fact that one "account for spouses [...] requires two email addresses and two mobile phone numbers" (IP4).
In summary, there are "subtleties" where the whole product still [...] needs optimization" (IP1).

## 5 Discussion

The intention of this seminar paper was to examine how the implementation of an AI, which delivers investment recommendations, in the area of asset management affects the organizational identity of a cooperative bank. Through the applied research, we were enabled to observe that there have been slight alterations in individual values of the bank, but that these have not influenced the organizational identity of the bank in any way.

Out of a total of 5 wealth advisors interviewed by the bank, only 2 advisors argued that the organizational identity has been positively alternated by AI. The shift is attributed to the quality of client consulting, but only described as a broader product portfolio. Thus, although a shift is discernible, this does not constitute a new or strongly changed identity.

A similar picture emerges when the negative alternation is examined. Only 1 consultant out of 5 has perceived a negative shift in organizational ideals. This mainly relates to the internal interaction with employees. As this is only mentioned by one consultant and relates to his colleagues, one can also not speak of a disruptive alternation in this regard.

On the other hand, if we draw the focus to no alternations, 5 out of 5 consultants confirm in several statements that there was no change in organizational identity through the implementation of AI. The 10 officially communicated values and also the anthropomorphic characteristics of the bank were only marginally affected. This clear picture is also supported by a finding by Mary Tripsas (2009). She posits that it is difficult to persuade the internal identity to change.

Based on the statements of all wealth advisors, we can therefore answer our research question "How does AI influence the organizational identity in client-oriented asset management?

We posit that this is due to the presence and relevance of AI for the advisors. This investment assistant is only titled as a support or even "satellite product" (IP5). Thus, the language already does not express high relevance of this AI. It should also be noted that although this AI is used by investment advisors, the stock and bond sector is not the only field of operation of these advisors. Thus, the identity of the advisors and the bank is not only defined on the basis of the stock market line of business, but also on the basis of loans and credits, current accounts, home loan and savings contracts, but also real estate consultancy. Hence, the organizational identity is distributed across a diverse portfolio of influencing factors. So if one area is influenced by an AI, the influence on the identity is nevertheless minor. It may also be related to the fact that the advisors mainly serve high-net-worth private clients and that it can be inferred from the advisors' statements that this tool is largely used for novices in the world of stocks and shares. If one relates this to an article in the Handelsblatt from 2017, in which it is claimed that around 50% of the money of wealthy families is invested in shares and private equity, as well as real estate (Narat, 2017), it can be interpreted that high-net-worth private clients already have experience with shares and the advisors are therefore not necessarily dependent on the tool and, due to the focus on affluent clients, also cover the segment of real estate and private equity. This suggests that these do not fit into the format of the inexperienced in stocks and therefore this AI does not account for a large part of the advisors' work. This conclusion further supports the ultimate conclusion that the AI introduced at this cooperative bank in the area of investment advice only affects such a small part of the advisor and the company that the impact on the organizational identity is far too tenuous to be able to ultimately influence it, positively or negatively.

In conclusion, it can be said that there are slight indicators for a possible alternation of the organizational identity, but the area of application of AI is too irrelevant for a whole identity change in the Bank itself.

## 6 Limitations and Future Directions

Our research is restricted due to several limitations. The interviews were conducted in collaboration with only one specific branch of the banking group and in addition, the AI is situated in only one area, wealth management. Therefore, it is possible that our findings are biased by time, region, branch, department but also by diversity and are subject to the characteristics of these influencing factors.

Due to our focus on this one branch, we were only able to interview 5 interviewees with the following characteristics. With an age distribution of 50-year-olds with over 60% of the interviewees, an average age of 48 years and a share of men of 80%, a clear picture of the interviewees emerges here and does not testify to a demographically diversified opinion. In order to be able to conduct more and more diversed interviews for future research, it would be advisable to conduct the next research across all branches within an organization. Also, since our interviewees all come from the asset management sector, it would be interesting to know how people from other areas of the bank would have described the organizational identity. Likewise, the decision-makers who decided on the implementation of AI could provide further relevant information.

In addition, the type of data collection, qualitative survey, is another limitation. Although personal interviews provide deep insights into human behaviour, the interviewers as well as the interviewees are often biased due to personal assessment and experiences. Thus, the vailidity of questions and answers can be eroded. In order to counteract this bias, an interdisciplinary research would be appropriate in addition to a quantitative survey.

Another limitation of our work concerns the timing of our research. Because the topic of AI is always being developed further and further, including our thematic AI, our results are tied to this technological state of AI. It is possible that as AI gains more functions and capabilities, organizational identity and advisors will be affected differently. In keeping with this theme, it is also worth mentioning that this AI is not disruptive, but only a supporting tool.

Finally, there is the possibility that a change in one of the factors just enumerated will also influence our surveyed result, and thus we can also come to a different conclusion.

**Appendix**

**Appendix I: Overview over the classified interview partner**
**In this case, IP means interview partner**

| IP [Interview Partner] | Gender | Age | Position | Employment |
|---|---|---|---|---|
| IP 1 | Female | 51 | Investment Consultant | 31 |
| IP 2 | Male | 56 | Investment Consultant | 40 |
| IP 3 | Male | 32 | Investment Consultant | 16 |
| IP 4 | Male | 56 | Investment Consultant | 40 |
| IP 5 | Male | 45 | Investment Consultant | 23 |

## Appendix II. Model of Codes; Gioia et al. (2012)

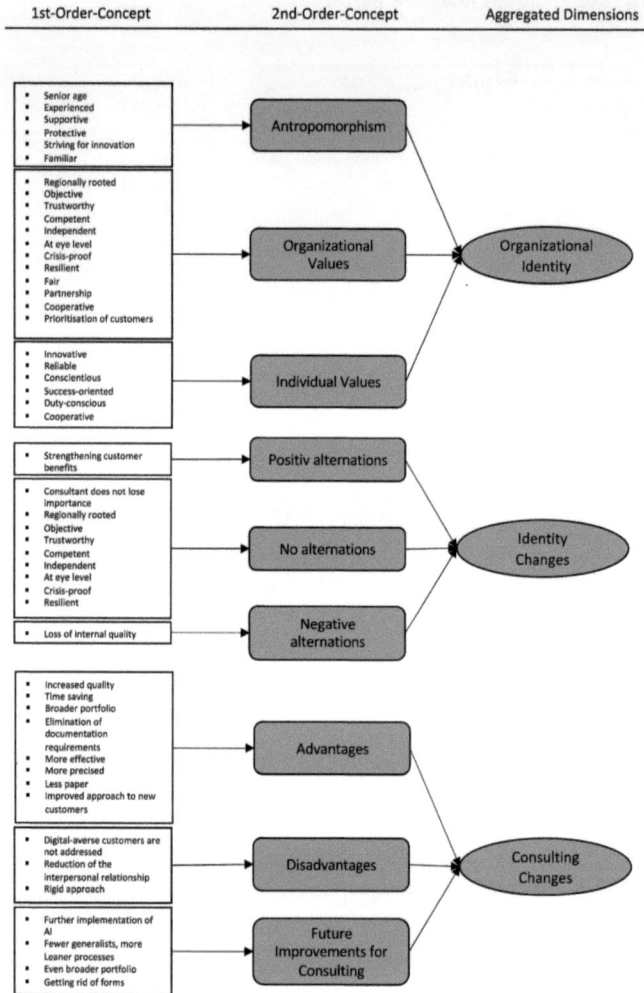

## References

Albert, S. & Whetten, D. (1985). Organizational Identity. In B. M. Staw & L. Cummings (Hrsg.), *Research in Organizational Behavior* Behavior, JAI Press, Greenwich, pp. (S. 263–295).

Ashforth, B. E., Schinoff, B. S. & Brickson, S. L. (2020). "My Company Is Friendly," "Mine's a Rebel": Anthropomorphism and Shifting Organizational Identity From "What" to "Who". *Academy of Management Review, 45*(1), 29–57. https://doi.org/10.5465/amr.2016.0496

Beineke, J. (2020, 19. März). *Microsoft Teams wächst durch Corona innerhalb einer Woche auf 44 Millionen User.* t3n Magazin. https://t3n.de/news/microsoft-teams-waechst-corona-44-1263956/

Brougham, D. & Haar, J. (2017). Smart Technology, Artificial Intelligence, Robotics, and Algorithms (STARA): Employees' perceptions of our future workplace. *Journal of Management & Organization, 24*(2), 239–257. https://doi.org/10.1017/jmo.2016.55

BRYNJOLFSSON, E., MCAFEE, A. & MANYIKA, J. (2014). Will Your Job Disappear? *New Perspectives Quarterly, 31*(2), 74–77. https://doi.org/10.1111/npqu.11457

.

Brynjolfsson, E. & Mitchell, T. (2017). What can machine learning do? Workforce implications. *Science, 358*(6370), 1530–1534. https://doi.org/10.1126/science.aap8062

Constantinides, P. (2019). Next-Generation Digital Platforms: Toward Human-AI Hybrids. *ResearchGate*. Published.

Davenport & Kirby. (2016). Just how smart are smart machines? *MIT sloan management review*. Published.

Faraj, S., Pachidi, S. & Sayegh, K. (2018). Working and organizing in the age of the learning algorithm. *Information and Organization, 28*(1), 62–70. https://doi.org/10.1016/j.infoandorg.2018.02.005

Gioia, D. A., Corley, K. G. & Hamilton, A. L. (2012). Seeking Qualitative Rigor in Inductive Research. *Organizational Research Methods, 16*(1), 15–31. https://doi.org/10.1177/1094428112452151

Harvard Business Review Press. (2019). Artificial intelligence: The insights you need from Harvard Business Review. *Harvard Business Review Press*. Published.

Lebovitz, S. (2019). Diagnostic Doubt and Artificial Intelligence: An Inductive Field Study of Radiology Work. *Association for Information Systems*. Published.

Lee, M. K., Kusbit, D., Metsky, E. & Dabbish, L. (2015). Working with Machines. *Proceedings of the 33rd Annual ACM Conference on Human Factors in Computing Systems*. Published. https://doi.org/10.1145/2702123.2702548

*Union Investment Institutional GmbH: Malina - KÃ¼nstliche Intelligenz im Portfoliomanagement | Startseite*. (o. D.). union investment. Abgerufen am 5. Juli 2021, von http://www.union-investment.it/startseite-de/Kapitalmarkt/Malina.html

Narat, I. (2017, 17. Oktober). *Umfrage unter Vermögensverwaltern*. Handelsblatt. https://www.handelsblatt.com/finanzen/anlagestrategie/institutionelles-investment/umfrage-unter-vermoegensverwaltern-so-legen-reiche-familien-ihr-geld-an/20346808.html?ticket=ST-2994112-14TmPaWRU7Yd5VVZKSbm-ap3

Orlikowski, W. J. (2009). The sociomateriality of organisational life: considering technology in management research. *Cambridge Journal of Economics*, *34*(1), 125–141. https://doi.org/10.1093/cje/bep058

Scott, J. W. (2001). Fantasy Echo: History and the Construction of Identity. *Critical Inquiry*, *27*(2), 284–304. https://doi.org/10.1086/449009

Shrestha, Y. R., Ben-Menahem, S. M. & von Krogh, G. (2019). Organizational Decision-Making Structures in the Age of Artificial Intelligence. *California Management Review*, *61*(4), 66–83. https://doi.org/10.1177/0008125619862257

Tripsas, M. (2009). Technology, Identity, and Inertia Through the Lens of "The Digital Photography Company". *Organization Science*, *20*(2), 441–460. https://doi.org/10.1287/orsc.1080.0419

Tyworth, M. (2014). Organizational identity and information systems: how organizational ICT reflect who an organization is. *European Journal of Information Systems*, *23*(1), 69–83. https://doi.org/10.1057/ejis.2013.32

von Krogh, G. (2018). Artificial Intelligence in Organizations: New Opportunities for Phenomenon-Based Theorizing. *Academy of Management Discoveries*, *4*(4), 404–409. https://doi.org/10.5465/amd.2018.0084

*Wertpapierhandel Dokumentieren*. (o. D.). IHK Lüneburg-Wolfsburg. Abgerufen am 5. Juli 2021, von https://www.ihk-lueneburg.de/produkte/beratung-und-service/unternehmensfuehrung-bwl/branchenspezifische-infos/anlagevermittler-und-berater/neue-protokollierunspflichten-fuer-wertpapierhandelsinstitute-ab-873172

Whetten, D. A. (2006). Albert and Whetten Revisited: Strengthening the Concept of Organizational Identity. *Journal of Management Inquiry*, *15*(3), 219–234. https://doi.org/10.1177/1056492606291200

Whetten, D. A. (2007). A critique of organizational identity scholarship : challenging
the uncritical use of social identity theory when social identities are also social
actors. In C. A. Bartel (Hrsg.), *Identity and the Modern Organization*(S. 253–
272). Erlbaum.

Whetten, D. A. & Mackey, A. (2002). A Social Actor Conception of Organizational
Identity and Its Implications for the Study of Organizational
Reputation. *Business & Society, 41*(4), 393–414.
https://doi.org/10.1177/0007650302238775

Zammuto, R. F., Griffith, T. L., Majchrzak, A., Dougherty, D. J. & Faraj, S. (2007).
Information Technology and the Changing Fabric of Organization. *Organization
Science, 18*(5), 749–762. https://doi.org/10.1287/orsc.1070.0307

# YOUR KNOWLEDGE HAS VALUE

- We will publish your bachelor's and
  master's thesis, essays and papers

- Your own eBook and book -
  sold worldwide in all relevant shops

- Earn money with each sale

Upload your text at www.GRIN.com
and publish for free